Let's read our feet!

By
Jane Sheehan
www.footreading.com

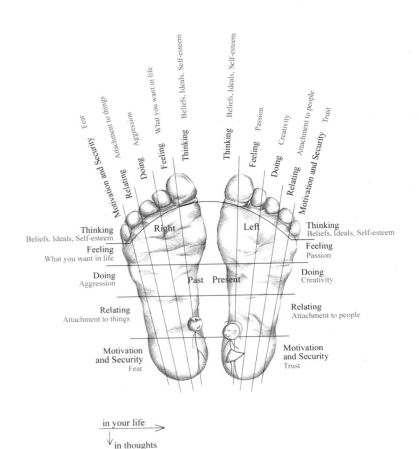

Fear
Attachment to things
Aggression
What you want in life
Beliefs, Ideals, Self-esteem
Beliefs, Ideals, Self-esteem
Passion
Creativity
Attachment to people
Trust

Motivation and Security
Relating
Doing
Feeling
Thinking
Thinking
Feeling
Doing
Relating
Motivation and Security

Thinking
Beliefs, Ideals, Self-esteem

Right

Left

Thinking
Beliefs, Ideals, Self-esteem

Feeling
What you want in life

Feeling
Passion

Doing
Aggression

Past Present

Doing
Creativity

Relating
Attachment to things

Relating
Attachment to people

**Motivation
and Security**
Fear

**Motivation
and Security**
Trust

in your life

in thoughts

"Let's Read Our Feet!"
by Jane Sheehan
First Edition 2005

Copyright 2005 © Jane Sheehan

Published by Jane Sheehan
Manor Beeches
Manor Gardens
Maids Moreton
MK18 1QA
United Kingdom

www.footreading.com

ISBN 0-9550 593-0-5

ISBN 9780955059308
(13 digit)

Illustrations, cover and layout by Redhead Designs Ltd
www.red-head.co.uk

Contents

INTRODUCTION

"Foot reading? How on earth did you get into foot reading?" That's what people often ask me. It all stemmed from when my friend, Claudine, asked for a reflexology treatment for her birthday. I'd never heard of reflexology and I thought it was a beauty treatment! To be honest, I was so cynical and down-to-earth that if I had known what it was, I probably wouldn't even have tried it. I booked her treatment and booked one for myself. From the minute the therapist touched my feet I was hooked. I had such a strong reaction to it. Every time she touched my big toes, I had tears streaming down my face. Every time she moved away from the big toe it stopped. It was the same on both feet. I had no idea why I was having these reactions but I knew I had to learn more.

I enrolled on a reflexology course and spent the next year studying how the feet have reflex points that can be worked to bring the rest of the body into balance. I learned all the physical parts of the body and how they were reflected on the feet. But at the end of the year, I only had a vague inkling of why I had the reactions I had. Furthermore, the clients I had used for my case studies all had emotional reactions that could be linked to the reflexes worked on the feet. I decided to spend some time researching more about the mind/body/spirit connection.

I read many books on the subject until one day I came across Imre Somogyi's "Toe Reading" book. Finally I felt I had found a clue to how my emotions are reflected in the feet. Then I found Chris Stormer's "Language of the Feet". This took the subject further and showed how the whole of the foot can be read. Once I'd finished these books, I then set about testing the theories on my friends and family. It got to the stage where when I entered a party, I'd have feet thrust before me before I could even get a drink in my hand!

Word spread about how I could see the personality on the feet. I was approached by a lady in the village where I lived to do foot reading at the local nursery school's fund raiser. I'd no idea how much to charge, or indeed, whether anyone would even be willing to part with their hard-earned cash in order to have a foot reading. The day finally arrived and with much fear and trepidation, I did my first paid foot reading on a stranger. When I'd finished, I looked up and saw that I had a queue of people waiting for my services. My career as a foot reader had begun.

HISTORY OF FOOT READING

People are always asking me what is the history of foot reading. I really didn't know so I asked some of the people who inspired me.

I asked Imre Somogyi who wrote "Toe Reading" where he learned it. He told me that he had developed toe reading himself. He had interviewed thousands of "victims", asking them about their behaviour and character. After five years, he and his wife Margriet produced a "Toe Alphabet" to describe the position and shapes of the toes and to link their findings to conclusions about character, personality and behaviour. He said that he got his initial ideas from polarity therapy and chakra therapy.

Chris Stormer who wrote "Language of the Feet" told me "Feet chose me…coming from a medical background, I was a total sceptic and wanted nothing to do with reflexology…but the Universe had other plans and, when I surrendered, I was given all the incredible Universal info, which I channel through."

Mosche Kruchik who wrote "Analyzing Personality Patterns Through the Feet" said "I do not really know what are the origins of foot reading. My knowledge about it comes from my training as a reflexologist and a lot from my own observation and practice. My intuition says to me that the Chinese are involved in this subject. They have complete codes for any part of the body – hand-reading, face-reading and such. Perhaps they were the first who dealt with this.….Who knows?"

Imre is Hungarian and lives in Holland, Chris is in South Africa, and Mosche lives in Israel but was born in Ecuador. Each of them have arrived at their method of foot reading independently. I believe that there is a history of foot reading in Iran, India and China and intend to visit those countries next year to research further. Perhaps that will be the basis of my next book!

From my own research, I have noted that the Chinese use a meridian system to chart energy pathways through the feet and these can be used to relate back to the person's personality. In India they have marma points on the feet that can relate back to the personality too.

To the people who don't believe that you can tell so much about a person through the feet, I would like to remind them that everything is recorded in the body down at cellular level. Nobel prize-winning scientists such as Candace Pert have shown that the mind and body are one.

WHAT IS FOOT READING FOR?

Foot Reading can be used as a party trick to astound your friends about how much you know about them just from looking at their feet. It can also be used as a therapy. In telling a total stranger about their personality and issues just from looking at their feet, you build a great degree of trust very quickly. With this trust comes responsibility. Words are very powerful and you must choose your words carefully.

You don't have to say what you see. If you are using foot reading as a therapy, you can read the feet silently to yourself, then use this knowledge to carefully phrase questions for the client to help them to arrive at their answers themselves. This is very powerful but can take a long time. I average 20 minutes for a foot reading where I say what I see, but in using it as a therapy where you ask questions instead, it can take up to two hours or more! Don't forget that you can use foot reading in conjunction with other techniques such as neuro-linguistic programming, self-actualisation, time-line therapy or counselling to help the client with any issues that arise.

My intention when giving a foot reading is to leave that person with something positive to take away with them. In looking at the feet, I am looking for the issues they are facing and want to leave them with some positive information that can empower them to help themselves move forward. How you choose to use the knowledge you learn today is up to you. I ask that you use it with love and kindness.

You are about to learn some guidelines that will help you to read toes and feet. There are times when you will see something on the feet that is not covered here. Given the techniques contained here, you will be able to make an educated guess about what it means by working out where on the feet it is and below which toe. When you explain to your client what you think it means and why, listen very carefully to their response. By remembering their exact words, you will then know how to read it when you see it again on another pair of feet. By listening to the client rephrasing what you say, you can fine-tune and improve your readings.

How do you feel about your feet?

The first question I ask when I see someone's feet is "How do you feel about your feet?" It's amazing what answers you hear to this question. People say, "I hate my feet", "I love my feet", "I feel cushioned" etc.

I say to you, how you feel about your feet is how you feel about yourself.

Listen carefully to how people describe their feet, the adjectives they use, and you gain an insight into their psyche. Before they even take their shoes off, you will already have clues about this person that will assist you with your reading.

Alex's Story

At a launch of a holistic therapy centre in Canary Wharf, I was chatting with my friend Alex, explaining about how you can know about the person before you even see their feet. I demonstrated by tapping some ladies on the shoulder and saying "Excuse me, we are doing a straw poll, can I ask how you feel about your feet?" The first lady said that she loved her feet because they carried her where she wants to go. The second lady said that her feet were OK but she wanted extra padding. I then told them that the reason we asked was because I was demonstrating that you can know about a person from how they respond to that question. I told the first lady that she was going places and her feelings about her feet reflected that. She was delighted and told me that she is amazed about how her career is going. She is a hypnotherapist and her career is going from strength to strength. I had to ask the second lady if she wanted more support. She explained that she had moved out of her apartment whilst it was being renovated and she missed it and was dying to move back in. She said she supposed that yes, she did need more support but once she was back in her apartment she would be fine again. I pointed out that she had used the word "padding" and wasn't it interesting that apartments are also referred to as "pads"!

You can see that by just asking another question can help draw out the person's feelings. When she first said "padding" I was intrigued and thinking of stuffing tissues down bras or wanting to be fat! I'm glad I didn't tell her my first assumptions and bothered to ask more questions based on what she said! The sad thing is, that by the time I'd discussed this further with them, Alex had wandered off so never got to hear the explanation about the padding!

ISN'T IT JUST MY SHOES?

When I am reading feet, I am often asked "Isn't it just because my shoes are rubbing" or "Isn't it because I wear stilettos?" Some women can wear stilettos for years and never get a blemish on their foot, others can wear them for one night and have callouses, corns or gnarled toes as a result. Think about it – you buy your shoes based on your personality. Some women buy stilettos because they love them and they feel good in them, others buy them because although they normally wear flat shoes, they feel they ought to for a special date. They aren't really being themselves and are behaving out of character. They are more likely to be the ones who get the blemishes. I'd still read the impact regardless of what caused the imbalance on their feet because I am looking at the effects of the personality on the feet.

SIZE MATTERS

Take a look at the feet. What size are they? Are they fat, thin, long, short? What are your first impressions?
Also, think about the common phrases in our language that relate to feet:

"Light on his feet"
"Toe the line"
"Put my foot in it"
"Getting cold feet"
"Shot in the foot"
"Best foot forward"
"Stand on your own two feet"

When you see a person's feet for the first time, if any of these type of phrases spring to mind, you are beginning to see clues about the person.

Carthorse

I think of wide feet as "carthorse" feet! This is a person who is always doing something – hard-working. They find it very difficult to sit down and relax. You offer them a cup of tea and they are already up out of their chair helping you by getting the cups and saucers out!

How would you help someone like this? You can't change a person. But you can offer suggestions. You could never tell this person to meditate because they can't sit still for long enough. But you can suggest they go for a walk on their own, concentrate on their breathing, maybe inhaling with two steps and exhaling in time to the walking. This in itself is a walking meditation to help them to relax and slow down their thoughts so that they can see what is really important.

Princess

Princess feet are narrow slender feet. This is a person who wants to be pampered. "Peel me a grape" types! That's not to say that they don't do any work, but given half a chance they'll delegate it to you! They find it very easy to relax. They're happy with other people running around after them. They like the aesthetic things in life. If you offer to make them a cup of tea they'd happily sit and watch you do it, and maybe say "don't put too much butter on my toast or my boiled egg will fall off". OK, maybe not quite, but you get the picture and if you had carthorse feet you'd probably already have the egg in the pan!

Long Feet

Even when you have finished growing, feet can still go up or down a shoe size. This is due to the tension or relaxation of the tendons and ligaments in the feet. Sometimes you will notice that it isn't the same for both feet. One may be longer than the other. Their right foot represents the past and their left foot represents the present, so you can tell them how they have changed from past to present.

Long feet show that a person wants recognition for their merits. They want to be noticed. Possibly hog the limelight.

Short Feet

Short feet belong to a person who is happy to stay in the background and watch and observe others before they join in. They don't want to be the centre of attention. They want to bide their time while they check everyone and the situation out before they make their move.

ARCHES

High arches are found on people who are very independent, have strong inner resources and find it hard to accept help from others. They need lots of time on their own to recharge their batteries. They like their own company.

Flat feet are found on very sociable people who don't like to be left on their own. They feel they need lots of support in life and are happy to let others help them.

You can sometimes see people who used to have high arches but the arches have fallen. Through questioning you will find that they have experienced a change in their life that has left them feeling that they need much more support than before. They may also have backache as this is often related to the fallen arch.

WHAT'S MY LINE?

If you draw a line from the little toe to the big toe, you expect to see all the toes meet that line. This is a person who is in balance, methodical and likes doing things from start to finish. This is the kind of person who would be horrified and personally affronted if you turned to the middle of a fresh notepad and started writing there rather than at the beginning. Of course, not everyone's feet are like this. First you need to understand how the energies work. Each toe represents a different area of the person's life. For these energies to come to fruition and meet the outside world, they have to travel through the big toe.

So when the big toe is much shorter than the line then you have a situation where the energies can not get lost. They are dealt with immediately. This is a person who is thinking twenty things at once and putting ten into action already! This is a real multi-tasker. They often work best in a support role. I once did a foot reading party for a group of nurses and each one without exception had this characteristic on their feet. That's not to say all nurses do. It's just interesting that this particular group all had this in common.

Now, let's take the case where the big toe goes well over the line. The energies can get lost before they ever see the outside world. This is someone who can be full of ideas but their ideas can get lost and don't all see the light of day. It would be great if they could have someone who picked up on their ideas and kept them focused on the best few! We'll do more about whether they are practical or fantasizers when we look at the shapes of the toe later.

The second toe can also go over the line. Many people ask me, what if the second toe is longer than the big toe. This is a trick question. Is the second toe longer or is the big toe too short? Remember to look at the line from little toe to big toe before you decide. When the 2nd toe is longer than the line then you have someone who has natural leadership qualities. They are able to delegate with ease. Watch out though - if they aren't allowed to be in a leadership role then they can become very bossy! If you are working with a group and you have someone with this type of toe, give them some jobs to do. Teachers, give this child the "monitor" role in your class!

If the third toe on the right-hand side is too short – the person is not keen on working to get what they want! If it's on the left-hand side then they don't have much creative energy.

It's less common for other toes to be over the line or under the line. If the fourth toe is, then I see someone who feels restless. The energy bubbles up but they don't know how to harness it so it leaves them feeling like they should be doing something but don't know what.

If the little toe is too short, then it can signify something that was traumatic that happened early on in life that made them have to grow up too quickly. The pay-back for them is that they maintain a child-like glee throughout the rest of their life. They love the simple things like butterflies, sunsets, jumping in puddles, playing on swings... Remember, be very careful what you say to this person because you are possibly opening a can of worms. It may be better to pose a question rather than to blurt out what you see. It may be better to say nothing. Trust your intuition to guide you on whether or not to say anything.

Little Toe Story

I once saw a 12-year-old girl's feet at an exhibition. She had a very short little toe on both feet meaning that she had had to grow up too quickly due to something traumatic in her childhood. I was surprised to see it on someone so young. She also had a verruca on the toe pad of the fourth toe. Fourth toe is about family and relationships and the toe pad is about thoughts relating to that. A verruca means an issue that is deep seated and starting to eat away at you. I discovered through talking to her mother that this girl's father had died. It became clear that she still had strong issues of abandonment to deal with. Armed with this knowledge the mother was then able to help her daughter further.

MEANING OF THE TOES

Learn this off by heart. There are many nuances once you know the feet well. But to help you, we need to simplify it so that you have a starting point. Each toe has a different meaning. The toes represent the person's thoughts.

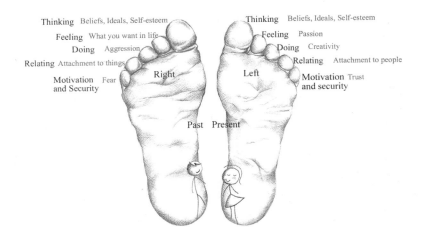

View of sole of foot
(that's why right and left are shown on opposite side)

You can then use this knowledge down the feet to show what is going on in the person's life. So not only can you read the zones vertically, you can read them horizontally too. Vertical zones represent their thoughts, horizontal zones represent how it is playing out in their life. For example, if something shows in vertical zone 3 and horizontal zone 4 then it represents their thoughts about what is being done or about work and how it is impacting their relationship right now.

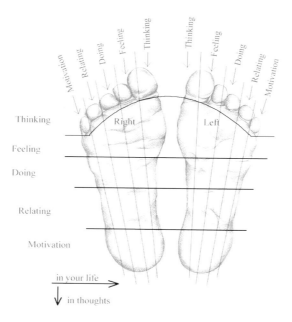

Right foot can represent the past and also male influences.
Left foot can represent the present and female influences.
Usually when I read the toes I don't make a differentiation between past and present. But when I'm reading the rest of the foot, I do if I see differences between the two feet.

The top of the foot is what is happening behind their back or what they want to show the world, the bottom of the foot is what is going on inside, what they keep close and don't necessarily want to show the world. Here, reflexologists have an advantage because they can also look at the health of the person because of their knowledge of the body map on the feet and can chose to read the feet in terms of health or in terms of emotion. For example, they can see the stomach reflex on the foot has a problem, so they can advise on digestion, or they can think that life is throwing that person "too much to stomach". If they see something out of balance with the spine they can see that the person needs more support in their life. If they see something wrong with the neck they can ask "who's being a pain in the neck". Hence, you can see that if you want to improve your foot reading skills further it would be very useful for you to have a reflexology chart.

Taking each toe in turn, let's look at them in more depth.

- Big toe – Thinking. The big toe represents personal beliefs and ideals. It's all tied in with self-confidence. It can show whether the person is a logical thinker or a dreamer depending what shape the toe is. We can look at toe shapes later.

- Second toe – Feelings. On the right foot, this toe represents what you want in life, on the left foot it represents your passion. How much of yourself you throw into life. Shape of toe is very important in reading this. Squeezed in the middle means they've learned they can't always have what they want and have to wait, but get there in the end. Narrow at the neck of the toe but wide at the end means that the person on the receiving end often gets more than they bargained for! Talk about a champagne cork going off! Possible drama queen tendencies!

- Third toe – Doing. Third toe is about action, the things you do, chores, job. On the right foot it can be aggression and on the left it can be creativity. There are often differences between these toes on each foot.

- Fourth toe – Relating. Fourth toe is about family, relationships, communication. On the right foot it's also about attachment to things. On the left foot it is about attachment to people.

- Fifth toe – Motivation. Fifth toe is about how you fit into your social group. It's about sexuality and security and personal development, about moving forward. On the right foot it can be fears and insecurities and on the left it can be trust issues. If the toe is looking outwards away from other toes, it is someone who doesn't want to listen to any outside authority – not what the teachers say, not what the police or government say. As far as they are concerned there is only one set of rules and that's theirs! They can be unconventional. If it is a straight toe then the person is more likely to be conventional and obey society's rules.

Later we'll look at the different shapes of toes and colours which will give you further information when viewed in conjunction with where they are on the foot. Memorise the above toe meanings to help you. However, for now it is worth noticing the difference between the base of the toe and the tip of the toe. If it is narrower at the base and gets wider at the tip of the toe, it shows someone who starts off tentatively but as their confidence grows, so too does the energy that this toe relates to. So for example, if the third toe is narrow at the base and wide at the tip of the toe, this is someone who is very cautious about the jobs they take on, but as their confidence grows in that job, they start to draw in more resources and make more efforts and as their confidence grows, so too does the project. When they complete the project, they look back at what they've done and think "My Goodness! Did I do all that?". They are amazed at how much they have managed to do and never would have taken the job on in the first place if they had known at the outset that it was going to get so big!

Similarly, if they have a narrow base of the second toe on the right foot and much wider at the tip, this is someone who starts off wanting something small, but when they go to get it, they come back with something much bigger. I usually say, if you went out for a sofa, you'd come back with a three piece suite!

COLOUR

Look at your feet. You willl see different colours tinging the skin. Using the following table you can start to understand what these colours mean. When you start to read other people's feet for them, keep your eyes on their feet as they consider what you are saying. You will see the feet start to change colour as they focus on what you are saying and as they start to connect to their feelings about what you are saying and how it relates to their situation.

Flesh coloured pink	Balanced and healthy.
White	Exhaustion, drained, washed out. Pockets of white, where it looks blotchy under the skin, can be anger bubbling under the surface.
Yellow	Fed up, bitter, jaundiced view, cowardly, cheesed off.
Brown	Browned off. This is worse than yellow but not as bad as blue/black. Don't confuse this with suntans! Suntans just mean they've been out in the sun!
Green	Envy, sick, jealousy.
Blue	Bruised feelings, low spirits, deep emotional hurts.
Black	Depression, black moods, deep emotional hurts.
Red	Depends on the depth of the red. Can be excitement, passion, or angry, embarrassed, agitation. A red toe that is flexible is a "toe at work". The person is going through changes relating to that toe, working things through.

When I give footreadings, I gain a lot of additional information from the colour changes on the feet as I start to question the person. Notice where on the feet the colour is, in terms of horizontal and vertical zones. This will give you additional clues. For example, I may notice a blue bruised colour on the relationship toe (4th) on the neck area, and I may say that I can see that they are having trouble in a close personal relationship (could be family, close friend or lover) and they feel hurt but are not expressing it.

As I mention it, they will start to think about the situation, and it is at that point that they access their feelings that their feet will change. I may see red start to appear on, for example, the 5th toe showing me that they are angry about the knock-on effect this situation has had to their feelings of security. In this way, by checking what changes on their feet as you talk, you can see more about how they are feeling. Don't underestimate the ability for the feet to change instantly.

GAPS BETWEEN TOES

Notice any gaps between the toes. Between which toes are they, and how wide is the gap?

Sometimes they are between each toe, sometimes just between certain toes, sometimes wedge-shaped and sometimes very wide.

Gap between big toe and second toe

Each toe represents thoughts concerning a certain area of your life. Imagine all thoughts and energies from each of the toes having to pass through the next toe and out through the big toe before it can see the light of day. If you can accept this, then consider a gap between the big toe and the second toe. The gap represents the energies and thoughts taking much longer to reach the outside world. There is a delayed reaction between the logic and the emotion. (Big toe represents thoughts and second toe represents emotions). This person often wakes up the next morning thinking "why did I let them get away with that. Why didn't I say this.." etc. The bigger the gap, the more the delayed reaction.

This kind of person needs to learn to make more space to think before they make decisions. "I'll tell you tomorrow", "I need to check my diary", anything to make space for them to seriously consider things and give them time for their emotions to catch up.

Often when a person has this gap and also the big toe is bent towards the little toe, they are the kind of person who feels that they can't ring up the next morning to cancel what they've agreed to do, because they don't want to let other people down, even when it means that they are not happy doing it. Where did they learn that? Isn't it better that someone else who wants to do it takes their place so that a better job is done. Isn't it more of a disservice to do something half-heartedly?

Gaps between all the toes

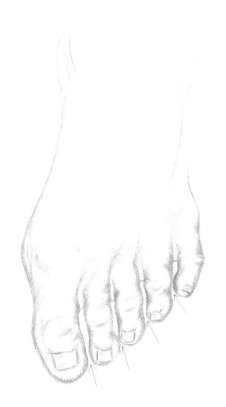

Little gaps between every toe show that although the person makes an immediate decision, they then spend a lot of time procrastinating over whether it was the right decision to have made, going over it again and again in their mind afterwards! There are constant reconsiderations and uncertainty. I tell them to take note of what the Cheshire Cat says in Alice in Wonderland. "It doesn't matter which direction you take, you always end up somewhere". Maybe not where you intended, but you can always take another path when you get there!

V-shaped wedges between all toes indicate that the thinking process elapses very slowly. This person can't be impulsive. They think, act or feel at one removed. I heard one girl say "I need to go home to look after the dog, he hates the lightning". Her v-shaped wedge indicates that it was more likely she who was afraid but she was expressing it once removed.

If there are gaps only between two toes, consider what those toes represent and interpret accordingly. For example, a gap between 2nd (emotion) toe and 3rd (work) toe on right (past) foot but not left (present) foot could mean someone who used to hate what they were doing, hence they kept their emotion away from work to force themselves to do something they disliked, but something has changed and now in the present they like what they do.

Gap between 3rd and 4th toe (work and family) could mean the person is trying to compartmentalise, keeping their work life and family life separate.

Karen's Story

Karen tells the story about her foot reading:

"After hearing about foot reading from a friend, I was keen to see Jane to see what it was all about. Jane spent a few moments looking at my bare feet without speaking and I was dying to talk to her but she seemed so deep in thought. Then as she talked, I was amazed that she could know so much about my personality by looking at my feet. Some of the things she told me I was already aware of and some not, and some were things about myself I had never shared with another person, not even good friends or family. When she looked at the gaps between all my toes and the pronounced gap between the big toe and second toe, she told me that I had a tendency to spend a lot of time thinking about what I would say or do, but not take any action at that moment in time. She suggested that people may take this lack of decision making as being indecisive or unsure. This is very true, and I have found this part of my personality really frustrating, at work and socially. Jane explained that this part of my personality was reflected in the gap that appeared between the toes. I asked Jane if I spend some concerted effort in trying to change, would this be reflected in my feet. She said it would and I could look at my feet and see the change.

I did make a real effort to give my opinion as it came into my head and not mull it over, to make sure I had thought about all the options. It was hard at first as I had acted this way all my life. However, it is getting easier and I feel more comfortable in saying what I think in the moment and not continually considering issues or problems. The gaps between my toes have closed up considerably. On a good day when I am feeling very confident, the gap is hardly there. On other days it is slight but nowhere near the size it used to be.

I have a lot more respect for my feet since meeting Jane. When I notice any changes like hard skin, callouses or changes in my toe nails, I now know what this means and I have a better understanding of my mental state and attitude."

WEBBED TOES

When toes are webbed, the energies of those toes are working together very closely. They can't be separated. The most common is a webbed 2nd and third toe. When you see this, you remember the 2nd toe is feelings and 3rd toe is doing. If this person doesn't feel like doing it, hell and high water ain't going to make them do it! The best way to reach this person is to appeal to their passion. They are very good at doing exactly what they want, when they want and probably frustrate others around them who may have a different agenda!

BUNIONS

You often see the big toes bending over backwards. This is representative of someone who is doing too much for others and not enough for themselves – bending over backwards for others. They need to learn to say 'no' more often. The bigger the distance off centre the more the person is out of balance. They are naturally motivated by helping others but have gone a bit too far. Put the feet together and check out the angle between the centre and where the big toe has bent to. Sometimes you'll notice a difference in the angle between right foot and left foot. You can see from this whether they've got better or worse by remembering that the right is past and the left is present.

TEMPERATURE OF THE FEET

Notice the temperature of the feet.

Hot	Angry, fuming, moving forward recklessly without a view to the consequences of their actions. "Hotfoot it out of there".
Cold	Think of the phrase "Getting cold feet" – they start, but don't finish projects, unexcited.

Sometimes it's just a part of the foot that's got a temperature difference. Note the area to get a clue about the person. For example, is it the heels (motivation or security) or is it the ball of the foot (emotions).

SKIN

Skin represents our reaction to life. Think of the phrase 'getting under my skin'. Any differences of the skin of the feet can show you what's happening with that person. The first place the body detoxes is through the skin.

I find one of the most amazing things about skin is that in 6 months' time every skin cell in your body will have been replaced with a new one, yet the callouses and corns and blemishes will remain. Our cells seem to have a memory. If you can release the emotional issue, you can see changes on the skin as a direct result.

Remember also to take note of the vertical and horizontal zones where this appears on the feet. This will give you an idea of what the issue is behind the emergence of the imbalance showing on the skin.

Callous	Protection against the outside world or concealing and protecting true emotions from the self.
Corn	Similar to callous but relates to a specific issue. Note where they are on the feet. Protecting ideas from being trampled upon. Inability to release past emotional issues.
Flaking	Extreme irritability.
Peeling	Shedding protection because issues are resolved - possibly because the person is ready for a new beginning or phase in their life. When it peels off in one sheet of skin it is about a fresh start, a new beginning.
Constantly Peeling	Trying to let go but the issues are not fully dealt with. Perhaps it might be worth seeing a counsellor or hypnotherapist for an objective perspective.
Cracked	Feeling divided. Often seen on the heels – where it represents obstacles that have to be overcome before you can move forward/feel secure. Look at which zone it is to gain extra clues.
Transparent	Vulnerability.
Rough	Having a rough time.
Moisture	Releasing fears at a deep level. The first place the body detoxes is through the skin so this can also be an indicator of someone who has abused alcohol or drugs depending on the severity of the moisture.
Sweaty/Smelly	This is what I call the 'skunk' effect! You are trying to drive people away so you can get your own space. You want more freedom. Often seen in teenagers who are put under too many rules or women who are carers of an elderly infirm parent.
Veruccae	An issue that has got so bad it is eating away at you. Look at which zones on the feet it is in to help give an idea of what the issue may be. It's deep rooted.
Athlete's foot	Extreme irritability that gets under the skin. Others constantly interfere, doubt and question your ideas, hindering your progress.
Warts	Subconscious projections of intense dislike, fears and repulsiveness.
Blisters	Constant emotional friction. Rubbing up against others' ideas and belief systems.

Callous Story

I attended a party once where a group of ladies had gathered to purchase items in the comfort of someone's home. At the party, a lady approached me and asked me if I'd mind having a look at her feet because she'd had a corn on it that she'd not been able to get rid of. It had been there for years. She'd been meaning to ask me at the last fund-raiser I'd done but I'd been fully booked and the opportunity hadn't arisen. So I had a look at her feet.

On her right (past) foot, below the 4th (family and communications) toe on the ball of the foot (emotions as they are playing out in your life now) she had a huge callous that had turned yellow and had a crater formed in the middle. I could see it was thoughts to do with a family issue that had not been fully resolved and were now affecting her emotional life as a result. She'd tried to protect herself but was fed up (yellow) at having to protect her emotions and now it was eating away at her (crater). It was well overdue for resolution. I decided to take the question and answer approach. I asked her how long she had had this. She explained that it had been there since her daughter was born six years ago.

On further questioning, she explained that she's normally the type of person who would weep at movies over the slightest thing and was very emotional and sentimental. When her first child was born she'd therefore expected to feel a lot of emotion, but when they'd handed her child to her at the hospital for the first time after the birth, she didn't feel anything. She felt numb. When the second child was born, it was completely different and she experienced all her feelings and emotions, but felt guilty about the difference in reaction from the first birth.

By this time, everyone at the party had stopped what they were doing and were listening. One by one, they started to share with her their experiences of birth and post-natal depression. It was a very warm and supportive atmosphere and I feel the lady had a lot of love and support and help from their sharing. All this time, I'd had one finger over the calloused area. As I took my hand away, someone behind me exclaimed that the callous had reduced. Indeed it had not only reduced in size, but the crater had gone and the colour had changed from yellow to red.

I understand that this lady was very emotional afterwards and did cry for a few days. However, the callous was reduced within 3 days to the tiniest speck. In releasing the blocked emotions, the feet were able to return back to balance.

Verruca Story

I'd been giving foot readings at a restaurant in Aylesbury that held themed evenings. The theme was of a psychic supper. When the diners were eating in the restaurant, there was a clairvoyant who gave a floor show, whilst I was in an adjoining room giving foot readings. I had the good fortune to be able to see a whole family's feet. I love seeing groups of family or friends or work colleagues as you can often see a theme running through their feet.

In this case, I'd seen both the mother's and father's feet and was about to read their son's feet. I'd already learned of the illness of the mother's father and that it was expected that he would not recover. When the son removed his shoes and socks, I could immediately see how this was impacting him. He had feet that turned inwards indicated that he was quite shy and introverted. He tended to walk on the outside edge of the feet. He had verrucae on the ball of the foot underneath the fourth toe, on the heel underneath the fourth toe and on the ball of the foot underneath the 2nd toe.

I read this as meaning he had a family/communication issue that was really affecting his emotions to the extent that it was eating away at him. He had issues relating to his own feelings of security also relating to this family issue and it was also affecting his emotions. I asked him about his granddad. I asked if he'd had chance to talk with him about his illness and if he had told him how he felt about it. We had a long chat about what it meant to him and he decided that he would ring his granddad up the following day to tell him how he felt. After the reading, I told his mother that the main issues related to his feelings concerning what was happening with his granddad and that it would be useful if they could talk with him about how he was feeling. Because he was such an introverted boy, no-one had realised how much he was affected by it.

Three months later I saw the whole family again at another psychic supper evening. The change in all of them was incredible. Their feet looked so different. And best of all, the boy didn't have a single verruca showing.

Wart Story

Not all foot readings are happy ones. I remember seeing a young teenager once who had the biggest cluster of warts under the ball of the foot under the big toe. To me this represented feelings of intense dislike of the self, feelings of repulsiveness. (The big toe represents self-confidence, personal beliefs, self esteem.) The fourth toe was completely clawed on the left foot indicating that in her relationship (fourth being attachment to people) she was holding in all her thoughts and feelings. I thought whoever she is dating, it's a completely destructive relationship for her and is ruining her self-confidence and self-worth. I'm afraid that I was completely unprofessional and told her that whoever he is she should dump him. I'm afraid it's not an approach I advocate and it was just because I was so shocked by her feet that I said it before I had chance to filter my reaction. Consequently, I only managed to upset her further, compounding the problem. As far as I know, she is still with him today.

I mention it here not just as an example of how to read warts, but as an example of how important it is to use the knowledge you have diplomatically and with great care. If I could take back my words and relive the experience I would handle it completely differently.

Cracked heels Story

Just after the war in Iraq, the doctors noticed that there were a large number of soldiers suffering from deep cracks in their heels. They were in dry desert conditions, drinking plenty of water, and there were no signs of bacterial infection to explain why this was happening. In some cases it was so severe that the soldiers could not wear their boots. Whilst there was no medical explanation for this physical phenomenon, I believe that it can be explained in terms of the emotions. In footreading, the cracks in the heels would represent the insecurities and obstacles that the person perceives they would have to overcome before that person could feel safe again. Further interpretation can be gained by knowing under which zone the cracks were situated.

NAILS

The nails represent protection of beliefs and ideas.

Big toe nail	Protection of beliefs, personal ideals, intuition, and thoughts
Second toe nail	Protection of thoughts regarding feelings, emotions and unconditional love
Third toe nail	Shields perceptions about activity and control
Fourth toe nail	Protection of thoughts regarding communication and relationships
Little toe nail	Protection of thoughts regarding expansion, mobility, security

Note that if the nail does not cover the whole width of the toe, the exposed area represents the degree of vulnerability on those issues. The upside of this is it also shows their degree of sensitivity too.

Thick	Extra protection of thoughts to avoid outside interference. Trying not to let others influence their thoughts
Yellow	Fed up at having to protect and justify ideas
Fungal	Extra protection is required because the person feels vulnerable and taken advantage of.
Split nail	Feeling divided and undecided about which thoughts to protect – their own or others? Wanting to stop pleasing everyone.
Bruised	Unhappy about having to guard decisions and hurt about having to protect own thoughts/ideas
Ingrowing	A deep need to protect ideas. Going to extreme measures to protect ideas. Thoughts threatened and vulnerable. Can also be hanging on to an out-moded set of beliefs when experience is showing you the contrary to be true.
Torn nail	You've been tearing strips off yourself – too much negative self-talk. Self critical. Revealing vulnerability.
Nail missing	No protection of thoughts. Feeling vulnerable and exposed. Lacking the substance or strength to back own thoughts and ideas.
Depressed nail (like pressed in the middle)	Lack of strength to defend personal decisions
Involuted nail (hollow underneath)	Making space to explore own ideas. You are avoiding the need to defend ideas at this stage whilst you have space to think them through properly
Ridged Nails: Horizontal ridges	Horizontal ridges indicate periods of dis-ease (stress) and vulnerability or emotional trauma. Consider the nail to represent one year. If the ridges are halfway up the nail the emotional trauma was 6 months ago. The new nail growth represents the present and the tip of the nail, one year ago.

ANGLES OF THE FEET

The right foot represents the past or male influences, the left represents the present or female influences. When you are relaxed and lying down, your feet will naturally fall into a position. You can read this position.

	Right Past	Left Present
Natural angle. Live for the here and now. Relaxed and balanced		
Exhausted and weighed down. Significant past issues need to be acknowledged to prevent tendency to look ahead		
Holding back something in the past but on track in the present		
Being held back because living in the past. Need to let go to live in the present		
Present progress temporarily inhibited because living in the past or looking back into the past for a solution to the present situation		
Addressing past issues in the present. Looking for solutions		
Wanting to move ahead. Living in the future		
Drawing in to the self during periods of uncertainty, insecurity or depression. Lack of self confidence. Introverted		
Soles that turn in to face each other (as if the person only walks on the outside edge of the foot) are particularly common in autistic people – representing an internalisation of thoughts and feelings.	Pronated feet (curved so the soles of the feet are trying to face each other)	

MEANINGS OF TOE SHAPES

If you haven't already memorised the meanings of the toes in Chapter 7, then go back and familiarise yourself with them before reading this section.

Remember, when looking at toe shapes, to check in which zone the toe is, in order to interpret the area of their life that it relates to (thinking, feeling, actions, relating, security/motivation). Note that people can have a combination of different toe types. Sometimes the differences are very subtle. Take your time to compare the differences between the toes on the left foot and the right foot. Noticing these differences can also give you more clues to read.

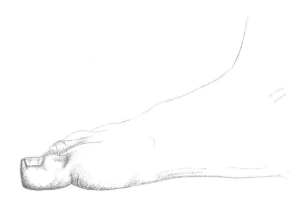

A blunt square-ended toe is usually found on someone who is blunt, direct, stubborn and often is (as one of my clients so nicely put it) an "immovable force". Once this person's mind is set, there is no point in trying to get them to change their mind!

A toe whose tip does not touch the floor yet the toe-pad is still in contact with the floor (not to be confused with a toe not touching the floor) is someone who can visualise, fantasise and generally escape into their head to escape their reality. If they can harness their visualisation then they can achieve great things because if you can think it, you can make it happen. Suggest that when they want to try new experiences that they visualise it beforehand so that by the time they come to live the experience, they feel they have already done it as they have rehearsed it in their head. (It makes trying new things much easier by harnessing their ability to visualise. They may not have considered using their innate ability in this way before.)

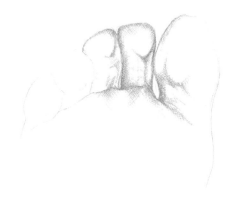

A drop shape on a toe pad shows extra hidden energy is being spent thinking in this area. These thoughts are going on behind the scenes and not revealed to the casual observer. Note which toe it is and thus work out the meaning.

A toe that looks as though someone has squeezed it reveals that the energy is stalled temporarily and there is no possibility of increasing the speed. On second toes it is as if the person realises they have to wait before they can get what they want. If it is on the work toe (third toe) it's as though, although initially enthusiastic, they curb what they do for a while. Note that this assumes the squeeze is in the middle. If the squeeze is near the neck area then it can mean not talking about issues relating to that toe.

If a toe is twisted, there has been a change of direction en route. The original energy was a recognised reaction, but by the time it has been expressed and the outside world receives it, it doesn't represent the original energy/reaction any more. The original reaction is presented as if from another source.

I've not actually seen this one before, so I'm just offering you what I've read about it. I would imagine if the fear toe (little toe on right-hand side) is twisted in this way, they would be the type to laugh during horror movies when they actually feel scared! If you find someone with this toe, please check with them and let me know your findings.

If a toe is bent at the end joint then it means the outside world doesn't receive the intended message. The message is received differently than was originally intended. For example, if the big toe has a change of direction at the end joint then it means the person tries to explain their beliefs or ideas but the person listening keeps getting the wrong end of the stick no matter how much they try to explain themselves. If you have this kind of toe it is a good idea to obtain regular feedback from your listener in order to avoid misunderstandings.

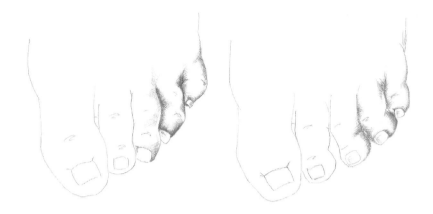

If a toe is leaning towards the big toe then the person is looking back at the past, comparing what was happening in the past to what is happening now. If the toe is leaning towards the little toe then they are in a rush, looking to the future, the next step. Again, read which toe it is to get a full meaning.

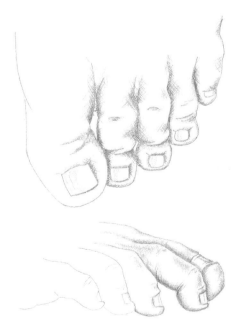

Toes that are withdrawn yet flexible and that rearrange themselves to the line from big toe to little toe, indicate a capacity for manipulation, for biding their time to present their ideas at the optimum moment. This type of toe usually has a prominent crease at the last toe joint (the one nearest tip of toe).

The extent to which a person can manipulate or postpone statements/announcements can be seen in the ability or lack of it to withdraw the toe.

Manipulative Toes Stories

Again, it is really interesting to note the differences from right to left foot. I met a TV presenter who has "manipulative" type toes on 2nd and 3rd toes on the left foot, but not on the right foot. I told him he used to be very open with feelings and work, but something had changed and now he bides his time, manipulating the work situation for his own ends and that this had had a knock-on effect on his emotions. He admitted that it wasn't comfortable for him but that he had to do this as he wanted his partner to conceive at a time when he could be there for the birth, so he had to be very careful about his work commitments so that he could ensure he would be there when the time comes.

On a different occasion, I met a nurse who had the manipulative toes on 2nd, 3rd and 4th toes on both sides. I told her what it meant and she went away rather miffed at being called manipulative (and who wouldn't be). I'm afraid it was another case when I wasn't careful about how I phrased what I said. However, she contacted me some time later to book a foot reading party for her friends. She told me that she had thought about what I had said and had observed her own behaviour for a period of time. She had decided that perhaps she could be less manipulative and could take a different approach to the way she handled her staff at the hospital. She showed me how her feet had changed. Sure enough, the creases in the toes were less marked and the ability to pull back and push forward had significantly reduced.

A toe that is tense and red indicates that there is a big change taking place, an effort to change a pattern or thought process. Which toe is it? This will give you clues as to which area of their life is affected.

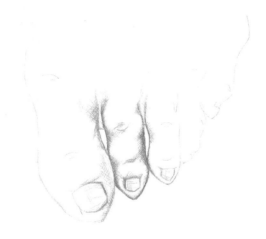

A pointed toe tip shows a person who expresses themselves sharply. They can be quite incisive. What they say may be unexpectedly harsh like a bolt from the blue. Not all toes will have this shape so you can read which toe it is to know what subject area they will express sharply.

Often in mothers with small children you can see this on the fourth toe – representing the family. Hence, though normally diplomatic, when it concerns the family she can be quite sharp and cutting!

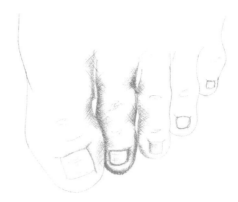

A rounded tip to the toe shows someone who is diplomatic and would be mortified if they ever said something to upset someone else. If you want to be mischievous, ask them why do they feel the need to please everyone!

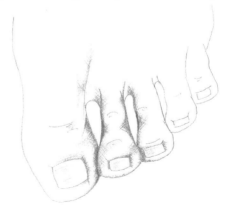

A toe that broadens towards the tip indicates an energy that starts off cautiously but that grows in confidence as the process progresses. For example, on the third toe, when they start a project, they start tentatively, but as their confidence grows they pull in more resources and the project grows with them. When they look back at all they have achieved, they are amazed at how much they have achieved. If they had known at the outset they were going to achieve so much, they never would have started it!

Note however, if this toe shape is on the 2nd toe (emotions) the person can be a bit of a drama queen! The emotion initially felt (indicated at the base of the toe) is magnified by the time the listener receives it (indicated by the increase in width at tip of the toe).

When the toe claws, the person is holding things in – either because the outside world has enforced restraint or because the person themself feels they don't want to express their thoughts/feelings for some reason. If all the toes are clawed, this is very sad. The person is holding on for dear life in every area. They are very repressed and probably quite anxious. Choose your words carefully. Why do they feel the need to hold things so close, not to release them? Why do they feel they have to carry such a burden?

A toe that does not touch the ground is not earthed. They are holding back their thoughts and don't want to come forward with them yet. This could be because they are biding their time or it could be because they don't know what they think yet. It's a way of escaping reality. They need to find a way to come back down to earth so that the energy can see the light of day.

On the big toe, this is someone who fantasises to escape reality. On the second toe, it is someone who doesn't know what they want in life. I ask them to explore what they want. What did they do when they were children in the school holidays? Ask them "If you had seven days to live, what would you do?" and watch for the answers that make them light up. If they can't think of anything, ask them to stay curious about the possibilities. When they realise what it is, they will find that the toe starts to connect back with the floor.

Emotion toe story

At a foot reading seminar I held, we chose a young man to be our guinea pig. He was reclined in the chair, presenting his feet to the rest of the class. I'd been teaching the class about how to ask open questions based on the clues that the toes presented and had explained that, as you talk to the client about this, if you watch the feet carefully you can obtain further information from their reactions to what you are saying. For example, if you talk about the relationship area, you could possibly see a change in colour on the fourth toe as they connect with what you are saying and experience their feelings about it.

So there we are, reading his feet. The class notice that his 2nd toes are not connected to the ground, but instead are held right back, in the air. I tell them to question him about what they see. The poor guy was bombarded with several people asking at once, in varying ways but with the same theme of "why do you hold back your emotions? Do you deliberately put off doing what you're passionate about or are you biding your time for the right moment? Why aren't you following your passions?" You can imagine, everyone talking at once and him not having chance to phrase an answer before the next question came.

Suddenly, one of the students exclaims that his big toe is moving, and sure enough, the big toe starts to move in front of the 2nd toe. Here was the clue that they needed. He was letting his logic take over from his feelings.

It was an exciting moment for them. They finally saw what I'd been trying to teach them – that by watching the feet closely when you ask the questions, you will get further clues to help you with the foot reading.

Interestingly enough, a student at this same event reported back to me some days later that they had seen a 3rd toe up in the air in a similar fashion. They quizzed them about their work and discovered that the person was having careers counselling because they didn't know what they wanted to do anymore.

Necks of Toes

The neck of the toes represents expression. If you view the feet from the sole, some of the necks are hidden. You can tell the areas of their life that they don't like to discuss with anyone. If the necks are very long, and visible from the sole of the foot then the person is good at expressing themself. Long and narrow necks of toes represent someone who is also good at creative expression. Wide and long necks of toes represent someone who is more practical with their creativity.

TENDONS

When you can see prominent tendons across the whole of the top of the foot it usually means that someone has been put under harsh discipline or a harsh regime. I saw this on the right foot of a 24-year-old man, but it was not showing on the left foot. He explained that he had been brought up in a strict religious household as his father was a preacher. He now lived away from home and was much more relaxed.

Sometimes you can only see a prominent tendon showing underneath the big toe. This represents someone who is very self-disciplined. Possibly rather too much so.

RELATIONSHIPS AND THE FEET

Once upon a time there were lots of fairy tales that had princesses lounging around in ivory towers awaiting their heroic princes to find a gap in their busy dragon slaying schedules to come and marry them so they could live happily ever after. I got to thinking about their relationships and how their feet would look.

Princess feet are narrow, representing the wish to be waited on, the ability to sit back and let others do all the work. The heroic prince probably had really wide feet representing someone who was constantly on the go, someone who can't sit still for a minute and needs to be doing something.

I hear the story of Cinderella, working from dawn until dusk, cleaning, cooking, sewing. I laugh at the thought of the prince trying to squeeze her feet into a slender glass slipper. There is no way that she would have had narrow feet. It's possible she had very short feet for her height, representing a wallflower type (someone who sits in the wings observing and biding their time before they jump into the fray.) I'm not saying this because of the old joke about women having short feet so they can get nearer to the sink, either!

My question is this – if Cinderella's prince knew what kind of woman he was looking for in a wife, would he have looked for a slender-footed princess-type or a wide-footed worker-type?

Many books on finding the right partner advocate writing a list of the character traits you'd like to find in a partner. When you meet a new partner you then spend some time trying to get to know them and checking whether they live up to your expectations. Then again, some people deliberately misrepresent themselves in order to manipulate the situation to meet their own ends.

What if you wrote a list of foot traits that you would like to find in a partner. Wouldn't it be easier to check his feet out? Think back to the fairytales. How well do you think the relationship would work between the narrow-footed princess and the wide-footed prince? There's no right or wrong. If the princess wanted to be waited on and have someone run around doing everything whilst she lounged around, it would be great. But the minute she wants him to stop and sit with her to watch a sunset or some other non-goal orientated activity, she would be sorely disappointed.

What about relationships. If you are looking for the ideal partner, perhaps you could consider their feet in conjunction with yours. Are you looking for someone with similar traits to you (hence similar feet) or are you looking for someone with different skills to complement your own? If it's the latter then you need to look at your own feet first to establish the type of person you are, then consider the type of foot that would complement yours.

For example, if you have "princess" feet – very narrow – and would like to let others run around after you, peeling you grapes and pandering to your needs, you couldn't go far wrong by choosing someone with wide "carthorse" feet. They would be happiest being busy and doing something all the time rather than sitting still and doing nothing. However, if you want someone who would be just as happy sitting still and enjoying the moment rather than being busy all the time then think again! How about a combination foot of princess on the lower half and cart horse across the top of the foot?

Do you value fidelity and loyalty in your relationship? If yes, look for someone who is completely unable to wiggle their little toe independently from their fourth toe! The toe reader, Imre Somogyi, did a survey of window dancers in the red-light district of Amsterdam. All of them except one couple could wiggle their little toes independently from the fourth toe. This couple only danced with each other and were only doing the window dancing to earn money quickly to achieve their dream of buying a farm in Australia. They could not separate sex from love.

A word of caution – just because the person can wiggle their little toe independently from their fourth does not necessarily mean they are a prostitute! It means that they can be fickle and need new challenges. They hate getting stuck in a rut and need lots of new challenges and interests.

Also, remember that people can change by choice. I have seen people who can wiggle the little toe on the right (past) foot, but not the left (present) foot. If I had a partner, I'd be worried if it was the other way round!

If you have a partner who can wiggle their little toe, then make sure that you keep them interested by constantly stimulating them with new ideas.

It's fun to read couple's feet together. You can show them the areas where they are the same and the areas where they differ and you can offer them a coping strategy to deal with the areas where they differ. It's far better to work effectively with the existing personality than try to change your partner!

GROUP READINGS

Once you've learned the art of foot reading, you can start using it in all kinds of different ways. Here's a few ideas

- Looking at the family interactions – who got which character trait from which parent
- What areas of your romantic relationship are in harmony and where do you differ?
- What are the potential strengths and weaknesses in a group?

One evening, I was giving a foot reading party to a group of eight women. Each of them in turn came into the room for a foot reading. By the time I'd done the 7th foot reading I was getting a bit fed up because they all had the same feet! Their feet showed they were all bending over backwards to help others, doing too much for others and not enough for themselves. They were all chaotic and deep thinkers, with good visualisation skills. I imagined them to be going back into the party and comparing notes and thinking that I was rubbish because I was saying the same thing to each of them. Then the 8th person arrived. I was so delighted to see her. I did her reading about how methodical she was and how well balanced. How she liked to do everything from start to finish in an ordered manner and how she preferred to work from the logical side rather than the day-dreaming side. How she was conventional and adhered to rules. I told her after the reading that I was so pleased she was there because up until her, everyone had the same feet and I had been worried that I couldn't do it because I was saying the same things all night! She laughed and explained to me that it was because they were all counsellors and she was the accountant!

That evening changed things for me. I started to take more notice of the interactions between the groups I was reading. How did their feet inter-relate? What were the similar personality traits and where did they differ. I began to notice that when it was a group of friends, there was usually a theme running through the feet. Whilst they may have quite different readings, there was usually a common thread running through the group.

Then I had the good fortune to start doing readings for groups of work colleagues, and again I began to notice themes running through people's feet who did different job functions. I saw a film crew where all the camera men had "workhorse, multi-tasking" feet. By that I mean they all had wide feet showing their need to be constantly doing things and an inability to sit down and do nothing for very long. Their big toes were below the line you would draw from the little toe across the other toes, which showed that they were multi-taskers, thinking 20 things at once and putting ten into action at the same time. The lady who organised and worked with them had princess feet which meant she loved aesthetics and loved to be pampered and delegate to all around her. She was in the right environment with all these "workhorse" feet at her disposal! She would have had them dancing to her tune without much effort!

I did a foot party for a group of nurses where the common theme among their feet was that they were motivated by helping others (most had bunions). Perhaps you could have guessed that without looking at their feet.

A very successful hairdressing salon contacted me for their staff party. I was amazed to discover that every one in the group except for one person had little toes pointing outwards, and in most cases the toe was completely on its side. When I see little toes like this it tells me that as far as that person is concerned, there's only one set of rules and that's their set! They tend to be unconventional and a tad rebellious! I had to admire the salon owner for her ability to manage such a group.

MEDICAL INTERVENTION

I'm often asked whether the personality or the foot reading is affected if someone has had a toe amputated or broken and reset. I'm afraid I haven't much experience of reading such feet but I'd like to include anecdotal evidence here. I feel more research is required before a definitive answer can be given.

Broken and reset toes

One bitterly cold evening in Aylesbury, I was at a foot reading party, reading my fourth client's feet of the evening. I had arrived at the stage where I would read the 4th toes. I was struck by the thought that her 4th toes didn't look right. On the left foot, denoting attachment to people, her toe had a slight curve towards the big toe, but on her right foot her toe was positively straight. But there was something about it that didn't seem right to me. I knew that I should read it as a straight toe but it didn't feel like that was the correct reading for her. I mentioned this to her. She enlightened me by telling me that she had had both her 4th toes broken and reset because originally they were so curved that they were underneath her 3rd toes.

I took the opportunity of experimenting to see whether the reading for the original shape was correct, or the reading for the current shape was correct. So for the 4th toe right-hand side, I told her that if it was straight then the meaning would be that she was very good at letting go of objects. Not very materialistic. I told her that if it was curved towards the big toe then it would mean she was a hoarder – having difficulty letting go of objects even when they were broken, in case they may come in handy later. I'd probably open her cupboard and have things fall on top of me. I told her the degree to which the toe was curved would show the degree to which she was unable to let go. By this time she has a wry grin on her face and she confirms to me that she is very much a hoarder and she hates to throw anything away. She's often chastised by her family for this.

I conclude from this example that in her case, the breaking and resetting of her bones has not changed her personality and that we must read her feet the way they were before the medical intervention.

I met a lady in London who had had her feet operated on surgically to correct bunions. She said they ran in the family and that despite three operations on the foot, it kept coming back. I told her what this means in terms of foot reading – that she was doing too much for others and not enough for herself. She laughed at this and agreed that this was indeed how she is. I asked her if her family who had the same bunions were also like this and she concurred that they were. Then I asked her what she would do if she could spend more time on herself doing something just for her. She thought for a while, then suddenly her face lit up with delight. She said she would do art and that she'd always wanted to do a history of art course when she was younger. It was lovely to see her so excited about something. I hope she does go and enrol because I know when she is doing what she loves she will make sure nothing gets in the way of that course and she will find her feet will change as a result.

Another lady I met in Ely told me she had had her bunions treated surgically. I saw that her feet had indeed changed and the big toes were nice and straight and central. I asked her if her tendency to do too much for others changed after the operation. She gave an emphatic "Yes". She explained that when she was recuperating she realised just how much she had been doing for others and how underappreciated it was, so she made the decision to change. She says she does a lot more for herself now than she had ever done. I'm still undecided as to whether the surgery changed her personality or whether it was her decision as a result of the recuperation from the operation that led to the change in personality, but I do know that if she hadn't made that change, she would have had to have more operations like the previous lady had.

HOW TO DEAL WITH REACTIONS TO READINGS

Giving a foot reading carries a certain responsibility. Sometimes you are saying what you see, but the person you are reading has been hiding their feelings or it is the first time they are hearing what they are feeling being said out loud. It can be quite an emotional time for them and sometimes you will have a client who reacts with tears. So how do you deal with this?

Normally when you see someone crying, you want to offer them a tissue, or give them a hug or pat their hand or some other such intrusion. However, this interrupts their body's ability to release what they are feeling.

As soon as you see the client having an emotional reaction, stop what you are doing and say something along the lines of… "I can see you are feeling emotional. Please shut your eyes and go into your body and tell me where you are feeling the emotion". They will then tell you from where the emotion is welling up. Next, ask them what colour it is and tell them to take their time. It does sound a bit strange, but invariably they do see a colour or colours. Once they have taken time to connect with what colour it is, ask them what shape it is. Is it jagged or smooth?

I would like to stress that it is very important not to attach any reason or meaning to the sensations that they are having. It is the mere fact that they are observing and getting curious about their body's sensations that is helping them to release the feelings quicker. If you attach a reason to it, it makes it stay around for longer.

Time and time again I have seen this method work incredibly well. It does go against the natural instinct to hold back and not offer comfort to the client, but to be honest, as soon as you start asking them these questions, their tears tend to dry up as they get curious about themselves.

Once they have tried this technique, you can encourage them to repeat the technique any time they feel emotional in order to help them to release it quickly and efficiently.

I've had clients who feel it in their throat, or heart, or stomach. I've had them see just one colour, or see several colours. I've had some just seeing one simple shape, or some seeing complex shapes like keyholes or head and shoulders. Sometimes the colours change as they focus on them. Sometimes they break up and move to another area.

For the people who have a colour or shape that they can not shift easily, I ask them to breathe in white light down to the area where they feel the emotion, then to exhale the colour. This is very effective.

When I see things on the feet such as the second toe not touching the floor, showing that they don't know what they want out of life, I often bring in other techniques and therapies such as neuro-linguistic programming, time-line therapy, life coaching skills. There are many ways you can use the interpretations that you have given a person to help them unblock issues. Remember above all that they are not broken in the first place!
The situation they find themselves in is perfect for them at that moment because it is the sum of the choices that led to it. It is the learning from their situations and experiences that is useful to help them to create the future that they want.

SEQUENCE OF A FOOT READING

First of all, there is no right or wrong sequence. I'm just going to tell you how I approach a reading and you can try it out for yourself. Remember that what is showing on the top of the foot is what they want the world to know, or what they perceive is going on behind their back. What is showing on the bottom of the foot is what is being hidden from the world or what is going on at a deep level. Reflexologists can also read the health of the person from the bottom of the foot.

To begin, I ask how they feel about their feet, then I look at the feet and gather my first impressions. I will say what my first impressions are. Then I work in the following way:

Starting with the top view of the feet:

- What's my line?
- Width and length (past to present comparing the two feet)
- Arch
- Toes starting big toe to little toe and comparing the nuances between the two feet. I don't read the toes as past to present, more as the nuance differences
- Zones over the top of the foot

Soles of the feet:

- If this is an exhibition or group situation, be careful what you say as the sole of the feet represents what is hidden from most people. The top of the foot was what they want people to know and what is going on behind their back.
- Work from zone 1 to zone 5 horizontally. Compare past to present.

To finish the reading, I keep a pack of Doreen Virtue's Fairy Cards and offer the client a choice of one card from the pack for guidance. If it is a foot reading party, I leave the booklet that gives the explanation of the card in the main room where the party is taking place so that they can read it there at their leisure and maybe make notes if they so wish. It's a fun way to finish off the evening. I remember one time when a lady begged me to tell her that she would win the lottery. She selected a Fairy Card and the card showed the words "Financial Flow"!

You can record the reading but if you decide to do this, remember to have the microphone nearer the floor as you will be looking down most of the time!

When you are still learning to do foot reading it is better to have a live subject so that they can give you feedback on how you are doing. Once you are better practiced, you will be able to read feet from photographs provided that the photographs are very clear. Before I hired my PR man in Hawaii, I read his feet through a photograph!

A FOOTNOTE

You now have the basics of foot and toe reading. You can now use your knowledge to help you to understand others better. But remember, with this carries a responsibility. You are to be as tactful and diplomatic as you can. When in doubt, express to the person that you are unsure then explain what you see and why. They may correct you with their own interpretation. Remember what they say and how they say it so that next time you come across the same thing you will be able to use their words to help the next person. In this way, you can refine your skills and your knowledge.

The information given here shows extreme examples. There are many subtle nuances to be seen and you may amend your reading based upon the other elements that you see elsewhere in the foot.

If you want to use this information as a therapy, then posing questions rather than saying what you see can help the person to arrive at the same place in their own time. I can do a foot reading in 15 minutes saying what I see and how I interpret what I see, but when doing the same thing by asking questions it can take hours.

Read your own feet before you practice on anyone else.

Seeing groups of friends at foot reading parties often shows up some surprising traits. There is usually a theme running through the feet of the friends. Seeing groups of professionals doing similar roles also can show a theme through their feet.

When you look at a whole family's feet you can see which traits the children have got from the mother or from the father. With some experience, you can even start to see the areas where they will clash and the areas where they will balance.

I hope that you enjoy using your new knowledge. I'm always interested to hear of any new or unusual findings concerning the feet and would enjoy hearing of your successes.

Further Reading

If you would like to read more about foot reading then I can recommend the following books:

"Reading Toes – Your Feet as reflections of your personality" by Imre Somogyi.
ISBN 0 85207 310 from The C W Daniel Company Ltd

"Language of the Feet" by Chris Stormer.
ISBN 0 340 64345 5 from Hodder & Stoughton

"Analyzing Personality Patterns Through the Feet" by Moshe Kruchik email carelife_israel@yahoo.com. This takes a different approach than taught here.

"Foot Reading" by Renee Tanner.
ISBN 0 9516203 7 1 from Douglas Barry Publications

Also, read the section on Skin in "Reflexology – The Definitive Guide" by Chris Stormer. Published by Hodder & Stoughton ISBN 0 340 62038 2. It's out of print at the moment so try second-hand book sections. She does intend to re-issue it soon so keep checking.